Singing Towards the Future

The Story of Portia White

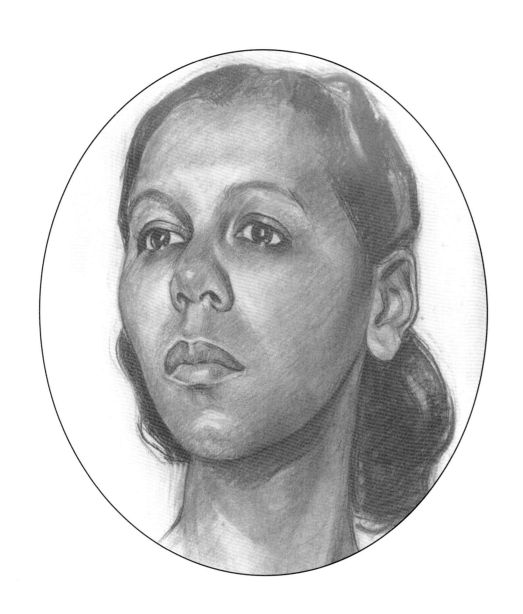

Singing Towards the Future

The Story of Portia White

by

lian goodall

Illustrations by Liz Milkau

Napoleon Publishing

Napoleon Publishing
Toronto Ontario Canada

Napoleon Publishing acknowledges
the support of the Canada Council for the Arts
for our publishing program.

Le Conseil des Arts   The Canada Council
du Canada   for the Arts

Napoleon Publishing also acknowledges the support of
the Government of Ontario through the
Ontario Media Development Corporation's Ontario Book Initiative.

Printed in Canada

08 07 06 05 04   1 2 3 4 5

Cover artwork by Liz Milkau
series editor Allister Thompson

National Library of Canada Cataloguing in Publication

Goodall, Lian
Singing towards the future : the story of Portia White / Lian Goodall.

(Stories of Canada)
ISBN 1-894917-08-1

1. White, Portia, 1911-1968. 2. Contraltos--Canada--Biography.
I. Title. II. Series: Stories of Canada (Toronto, Ont.)

ML3930.W587G64 2004   j782.42168'092
C2004-900048-9

To Aunt Anna, whose questions set me on the journey,
and to Derek, who embarked on the adventure.

Singing Before Royalty

Portia White greets Prince Philip, the Duke of Edinburgh after singing for Queen Elizabeth (foreground). It was one of Portia's last public performances.

Portia White stood tall at centre stage, her regal poise and charm enchanting everyone. Her beautiful vocal music sent a shiver of delight through the audience as they listened to the big voice with its famous clear bell-like tones.

Queen Elizabeth, Prince Philip and everyone in the crowd applauded at the opening of Confederation Centre in Charlottetown, Prince Edward Island, October 6, 1964. As the singer took her bow, she smiled with joy and happiness at receiving royal recognition.

Portia was the first singer trained only in Canada to reach an international stage. This Nova Scotian battled poverty and other troubles to become a concert star known across Canada, in the United States, the Caribbean, and Central and South America.

It had been a long, hard journey to reach the special event of singing at the Queen's command. This day had come after years of hard work and believing in a dream that seemed impossible. It was a dream that had begun many years before in a small town in Nova Scotia.

From left to right: Helena, Portia, Billie, Nettie, Izie holding Mildred, Romney

These are the children of Reverend William Andrew (1874-1936) and Izie White (1890-1972):

Helena Isabella (1908-1991)
James Romney (1909-1919)
Portia May (1911-1968)
Nettie Jean (1914-1979)
William Andrew (Bill) (1915-1981)
Mildred Elizabeth (1917-1980)
Milton Arthur (1920-1921)
George Albert (1921-)
June Aurora (1923-1994)
John Edgar (Jack) (1925-2002)
Vera Izie Evelyn (1927-1939)
Ronald Lorne (1928-)
Lucille Yvonne Grace (1930-)

Baby Portia

On June 24, 1911, a special baby was born—an infant who would grow up to become an important singer. Her achievements would help change the future possibilities open to many Canadians. Portia May White was born in Truro, Nova Scotia. She was the third child of Izie Dora and William Andrew White. As the Whites held their baby, they knew that she was their precious gift.

Her father asked his friend, Helena, for suggestions for his new daughter's name. Helena chose Portia after one of the main characters in Shakespeare's famous play *The Merchant of Venice.* Shakespeare's make-believe Portia was a strong and clever girl. How could anyone guess what a good choice this would be? Portia White would grow into a strong person who would work toward making her dreams come true.

Portia's Father

Helena Blackadar, a friend of Portia's father, named the Whites' second daughter. The Whites had also named their first child, Portia's older sister, Helena, after this woman. Why was this Baptist missionary such an important person in Portia's father's life? She was the one who suggested he leave the United States, where he was born, and study to become a minister in Canada.

William Andrew White, often called Andrew, was born in 1874 in Virginia. He was the ninth of ten children born to William and Isabella (Waller) White. His parents had been born slaves, Black people who were owned and controlled by white people. Owners could do anything to their slaves. They could sell their slaves whenever they wanted, as if they were horses. Families could even be separated.

Slavery ended in Canada and the British Empire in 1833 and in parts of the United States by 1863. William Andrew's parents had bought their freedom and were no longer slaves but landowners when William Andrew was born. No one could legally own slaves in William Andrew's time. However, this did not mean that the Whites' son lived in a world where Blacks were treated fairly. Young Black men such as William Andrew had fewer job opportunities than white men. They were mostly hired to do hard physical work as

Reverend William Andrew White,
Portia's father

3

BLACK IMMIGRANTS ACROSS CANADA

Many immigrants of African descent have contributed to the growth of Canada. The first Black person to set foot on what is now Canadian soil was Mathieu da Costa, who was in Samuel Champlain's landing party at Port Royal in 1604. In 1628, a British ship brought a six-year-old slave boy from Madagascar to New France. During the time that selling slaves was still legal, settlements of some freed American slaves were created in Wilberforce, Dawn, Elgin and Buxton, towns in Ontario. Between 1815 and 1860, more than 50,000 slaves escaped to Quebec, Ontario, and elsewhere on an "invisible train." This network of people and safe houses was called the Underground Railroad. On the West Coast, a group invited from the United States became some of the early permanent settlers on Vancouver and Salt Spring Islands. In Alberta, families of African descent made some of the first homesteads.

porters, barrel makers, steel workers, labourers or gardeners. A few educated Blacks taught in Black schools or worked as ministers.

Becoming a minister interested William Andrew. His parents were followers of the Baptist faith. Their son was eager to start studies in theology that would lead him to a career in the church.

Black Americans did not have as many places to go to university or college as white Americans. Helena suggested that William Andrew apply to a university in her home province of Nova Scotia, where Blacks were accepted. William Andrew jumped on the idea. He must have been very happy the day he graduated in 1903, only the second person of African descent to graduate from Acadia University.

William Andrew became an ordained minister and began working in different churches around Nova Scotia. Soon he met a lovely young woman.

BLACKS IN NOVA SCOTIA

More than 3,000 Blacks, both free and slaves, came to Nova Scotia after the American War of Independence in 1775. Those who stayed under British rule were called United Empire Loyalists. Most promises of free land made to Black Loyalists were not really kept. In 1792, a ship with 1,196 people sailed to Sierra Leone, Africa, where they hoped to build a better life.

Another group, proud ex-slaves known as Maroons, arrived from Jamaica in 1796. They helped build the Halifax Citadel, a famous fortress. Five hundred of the group of 600 left for Sierra Leone in 1800.

Once again, loyal people of African descent were promised free land during the War of 1812 between Britain and the United States. More than 1,619 Black refugees arrived in the Maritimes during this period.

Portia's Mother

Izie White had beautiful dark eyes and a warm smile. Like William Andrew, Izie also grew up in a large family. She was the tenth of the eleven children of James and Alicia (Taylor) White. Even though Izie had the same last name, she wasn't related to William Andrew White. Her family was from Nova Scotia, and one grandfather immigrated from England. Some of her ancestors had probably once been slaves in the United States. They moved to Nova Scotia many years before as United Empire Loyalists. Izie was also descended in part from people of the Mi'kmaq nation, one of the First Nations peoples.

In June 1906, William Andrew White married Izie Dora White of Mill Village, Nova Scotia. He was thirty-two years old, and Izie was half his age, not quite sixteen years old. They began a happy, loving marriage. Thirteen children were born to the Whites, although some of them died very young. Portia grew up as the third eldest, with seven other siblings—a total of ten children. There was lots of activity in the White house, and it was always full of song and laughter.

TRURO

The town where Portia was born is known as the "hub" of the province. Truro is in east central Nova Scotia, on the Salmon River, at the head of Cobequid Bay near the Atlantic Ocean. In addition to the community of African descent, Truro was home to an interesting mix of people. The first settlements along the Salmon River were encampments of the Mi'kmaq people. Some families had Acadian ancestors, people of French origins who were first recorded in the area in 1689. Others settlers in the 1760s had Irish-Scottish roots. No one knows where the name Truro comes from, but it is a town where many people felt happy to live and grow up. In 1999, to celebrate its heritage, Truro began a tree sculpture project. More than twenty artworks were carved out of tree trunks to honour important community members. One of these is Portia (see page 60). Another honouree is Chief Rachael Marshall, who was born in Truro two years before Portia. In 1969, she became Chief of the Millbrook First Nation and the first woman to be named to this position in Nova Scotia.

A Bright Little Girl

Portia's parents were proud of their bright little girl. Her mother thought she was smart when she learned to spell a very big word, "cosmopolitan," at a very young age. The word describes someone who is sophisticated and knows a lot about the ways of the world. Although she may not have understood the meaning, Portia seemed to love that word. She would boast to all their visitors "I can spell cosmopolitan. Listen, c-o-s-m-o-p-o-l-i-t-a-n." Izie said that the family was "glad when she found a few new words to pester people with." In the early years of her life in Truro, the little girl played and grew the same as the other children. No one could have predicted that Portia, one day, would become a cosmopolitan woman.

Music at Home

There was always music in the White home. Their wonderful, inspiring mother always had a song, even though she was often cooking meals for someone from the church as well as looking after her large family. The children were helpful, especially the elder sisters, Helena and Portia, as the younger ones came along. There was wood to fetch, clothes to wash, meals to prepare, and dishes to wash without the help of machines or electricity. Izie was usually wearing an apron and working. However, she was never too busy to share her special gifts—a caring smile and a love for music.

Izie had a beautiful soprano voice. She taught Portia and some of the others to play the piano. Most of Portia's four brothers and five sisters grew up with a fondness for singing and the ability to play an instrument. Singing was as usual as talking in the family. Whether they were doing dishes or setting the table, someone was always singing. Portia thought it was "a natural thing...a child bursting into song."

MUSIC WHEN PORTIA WAS SMALL

Music was a very important form of entertainment when Portia was growing up. Many people played instruments. They would get together with their friends and family to play and sing. Over the years, evenings of song happened regularly at the White home.

People also flocked to concerts to see bands and live performers. Some of the most admired entertainers were classical singers. When Portia was small, the music of famous classical singers was played on gramophones. In the 1930s, radio had appeared, but televisions didn't arrive until Portia was an adult. By this time, opera and classical weren't as popular as other types of music.

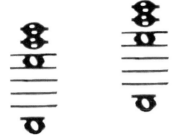

World War I

HONOUR BEFORE GLORY

Portia's father wrote letters home and also kept a diary which family member Anthony Sherwood has used to tell the story of the men of the Number Two Construction Battalion in an excellent video called *Honour Before Glory*.

Canadians of African descent played in army bands and made other wartime musical contributions. Hattie Rhue-Hatchet was born in 1864, the daughter of escaped slaves from Virginia who moved to the Elgin Settlement, Ontario. In Buxton, Ontario, she taught and wrote music. One of the songs she composed, "That Sacred Spot," was adopted by the Canadian troops in World War I as their official marching song.

When Canadian troops went overseas to fight for Britain, Reverend White joined the army. From 1917 to 1919, he served as chaplain to the Number Two Construction Battalion, the first battalion of Black Canadians ever formed. At first, white superiors did not think that Canadians of African descent would make good soldiers. There were no Black battalions (army units of more than one company) until the Number Two Construction Battalion was created and sent to France. There, the men cut lumber, built railroads and had the dangerous job of stretching barbed-wire across the front lines. Conditions were very difficult, and the Number Two did not receive the same supplies as other battalions, nor did they receive equal treatment. Reverend White counselled his men as best he could.

Reverend White missed his children terribly. Izie wrote letters telling him what the children were doing, and William Andrew wrote back. Some of his letters talked about the band that the soldiers in the Number Two Construction Battalion had started. Even in war-torn France, Canadian musicians of African descent were playing. Marching bands performed some of the most popular music of

Reverend White in uniform

the time. People loved hearing the music of brass instruments, such as tubas and cornets, with the thump-thump of the big bass drum keeping time.

At Christmas, William Andrew's letters spoke of visiting his men in the hospital and the turkey dinner the patients had. He described his own feast with the officers and nurses in the officers' mess. Reverend White would have been the only Black officer at the Christmas dinner, because he was the only Canadian of African descent to be made an officer in the army.

For the children, listening to letters was not the same as hearing the words spoken aloud by their father's powerful, yet gentle voice. Viewing a photograph of him, standing tall and looking handsome in his uniform, was not as wonderful as sharing a big hug and feeling his scratchy mustache. Kneeling to give thanks for dinner without their father was not as exciting as asking for a blessing with him for one of his freshly caught lake trout. The two-year separation was difficult for the entire family.

Move to Halifax

It was a happy day when Reverend White returned from the war. It was a joyful time until a terrible thing happened. Portia's brother, Romney, met with an accident. He died the day after Christmas, 1919, from head injuries that he received from being hit by a rock, perhaps when he fell off a wagon. From then on, the children were not allowed to ride on the back of horse-drawn wagons.

It might have helped eight-year-old Portia with the pain of losing her brother that the family immediately became busy with important changes. Reverend White took the job of minister at the Cornwallis Street Baptist Church in Halifax. The White family moved from quiet Truro to Halifax, the bustling capital city of Nova Scotia. First the Whites lived in a house right beside the church. They later moved to a home on Belle Aire Terrace, where the family lived for many years.

Cornwallis Street Baptist Church

CHURCHES

Churches have been important for Canadians of African descent as special places to pray, share friendship, help one another, join organizations and celebrate a unique heritage.

Churches also gave some members the keys to their careers. Young Black Canadians were encouraged at that time to have jobs that did not need much schooling. Many white people thought that they were suited for physical labour, not thinking. Ministers such as Reverend White, however, went to university and became respected leaders of their communities.

Many Black singers first sang in church choirs. Well-known American classical singers Sissieretta Jones, Dorothy Maynor and Carol Brice were also ministers' daughters who sang in church choirs.

Music in the Church

The children of this special musical family practised their talents at their father's church. Izie directed the choir and trained her children as choir members.

On Sundays, light streamed through the beautiful coloured windows. It bathed the decorations of flowers and the churchgoers. It seemed each week more people came to hear Reverend White preach. He was considered a strong and gifted speaker.

As Portia stepped forward to sing her solo, waiting eyes looked expectantly at her. The eight-year-old girl might have felt frightened, but her parents smiled encouragingly, and soon Portia's lovely voice joined the music. The sacred melody seemed to lift her above all the faces in front of her. Her heart soared happily.

Later in life, Portia glowed when she remembered Sundays at the Cornwallis Street Baptist Church. She laughingly recalled that sometimes the White family made up almost the entire choir. She smiled, saying that when the boys' voices were changing, the girls would have to take over their parts as tenors until another brother was old enough to join the choir.

RANGES OF SINGERS

Audiences loved to hear operas or recitals where the great stars of the day would sing solos or arias from operas. Women with the highest voices are called sopranos. The lower female range of singers are mezzo-sopranos and lower still, contraltos. Male singers are divided into tenor, baritone and the even lower bass.

It takes many years of study and training to become an opera singer.

Contests and Radio

When she was only eight years old, Portia and one of her sisters entered a music contest. They sang the soprano parts from the opera *Lucia di Lammermoor*. Portia was learning about opera, the music many people loved.

The young singer and her siblings also had other chances to perform. Their father was the first Black preacher to make radio broadcasts across parts of Canada and the United States. Younger sister June and Portia sometimes sang on their father's radio shows. Imagine how exciting it would have been for Portia to sing into a microphone knowing that her voice was travelling across the airwaves to people she couldn't see.

This was an important time. Portia was gaining experience, and she was beginning to have a dream. When she went to sleep, her mind would begin to plan. She would wake up knowing, "I had this dream. I was always bowing in my dreams, and parading before people across the stage."

Singing at School

The house on Belle Aire Terrace, where the Whites lived

LOVE OF BOOKS

Portia found happiness in the land of literature. Her ticket there was a good book, for Portia loved reading. Lucy Maud Montgomery was one of her favourite authors, but her mother said she would read "anything and everything that had print on it." Once William Andrew found Portia with a book which he didn't think was a good one. "It doesn't belong to me!" she explained, but too late. Reverend White had thrown the book into the fire. Although she wasn't allowed to read everything, Portia was "inside" a book so often that her family called her a "book worm." At four o'clock in the morning, Portia would still be up reading.

Portia went to Alexandra Public School in Halifax, which was an integrated school with both Black and white students. For some reason, Portia was unsure about singing at school. Singing with her classmates made her feel different and very self-conscious. It seemed to Portia that whenever she opened her mouth, the boys and girls in her class would look at her. She thought perhaps she was off-key. She did not know that the other students were impressed with what they heard.

Later, when she was an adult looking back at these times, Portia recalled some sad feelings. "I was always a little bit discontented when I was a child, not as happy as the others," she said. "I don't know why. I had lots of freedom and lots of company and I should have been happy. But I was always very tense and used to go around with a heavy heart. Perhaps," she concluded, "it was because I wanted to express myself but I didn't know how."

Naughty Teen

Portia (on the right) and her sister Nettie

Portia could be very naughty. One day, when she was a teenager, Portia and her brother, Bill, were home by themselves. Portia called Bill up to the bathroom, where there was a window overlooking the street. They could see a man wearing a hat coming down the sidewalk. They waited until the man drew near, then Portia poured a pitcher of water on his head. The man was quite angry and rang the doorbell. Portia answered. Acting in a very adult manner, she listened to his complaint and said, "That is terrible, sir. I will certainly see that they get punished."

Like all brothers and sisters, the White siblings sometimes had their tussles. Portia caught her sister Nettie writing nasty words on a fence and decided to blackmail her. From then on, in order to "buy" Portia's silence, Nettie had to hand over her dessert. As an adult, Nettie rarely ate dessert, probably because she had never had the chance to acquire a taste for it.

Bloomfield High School in Halifax

Finishing School

At Bloomfield High School, Portia disliked science and loved languages. She didn't know what she wanted to study next, although she thought about continuing in business studies. At graduation, the yearbook foretold that she would soon see her name in lights. Portia was passionate about singing, but planning a career as a concert singer was unthinkable. The most famous Canadian opera star, Emma Albani, had studied, lived and worked mostly in Europe. Portia could never afford that. In addition, there were no Black women in Canada who were well-known recital singers and very few in the United States.

Not many jobs were open to Canadians of African descent. Young men were told to study Shop (Industrial Arts) to prepare them for work as labourers—not dentists or scientists. Most women worked as servants of white people. The list of the careers which Black Canadian women were not allowed to follow was longer than the list of what they were encouraged to do. White women were becoming nurses, but Black women were not admitted to nursing programmes. As for a future of singing on stage? The dream was too daring.

EMMA ALBANI

Madame Albani was the first Canadian woman to be a famous international singer. Emma Albani was born Emma Lajeunesse in Quebec in 1847. After studying in Paris and Italy, she became a great soprano, an opera star. She was also a dear friend of Queen Victoria. Albani sang in some of the large cities in Europe. She toured in North America several times, returning to visit her native land. Canadians, especially French Canadians, always had a special place in her heart. Beloved in many countries of the world, Albani died in 1930.

SEGREGATED SCHOOLS

Although Portia went to integrated schools, Black Canadians could only teach in segregated schools. The laws which created separate schools for Blacks stayed in place until 1954 in Nova Scotia. Money for these schools came from the communities around them, and since Black parents were unable to access high-paying jobs, they could not give much money. Teachers had problems, as the schools were poorly equipped.

One teacher, Florence Bauld, received her teaching diploma in 1957 and taught at the Partridge River School for twenty years. She recalls that the community felt the facilities to be so bad that they complained to the Human Rights Commission of Nova Scotia against the Halifax School Board.

A Job, A Dream

Portia had to share the dream beating in her heart with someone. Portia told her father that she wanted to sing, "Not just sometimes, but to live by singing, to sing with the freedom and power that a flier feels in the sky." Reverend White thought at first that she meant to be a blues singer and felt that sort of singing was more like wailing. But Portia explained that her interest was classical music, music he respected.

Reverend White knew that music lessons took money, and that most singers went to Europe to train further. Ministers were not paid well, and William Andrew had a large family. He worried that he couldn't help her much.

"Oh, no! Father, I'll take the job teaching. I'll work and save and study," Portia enthused.

"That's my girl!" Her father seemed convinced. "There are no barriers between you and your heart's desire," he is said to have told her. "Be a big singer, Portia. Make your people mighty proud."

Teacher

Portia attended Dalhousie University in 1929 and then found a teaching job. She needed money to live and for her musical studies. She was eighteen years old.

Portia taught at a number of schools for Black students in the Halifax area: Lucasville; the Nova Scotia Home for Colored Children in Dartmouth (a home for orphans); Beechville and Africville.

Africville, just outside of Halifax, was founded by ex-slaves after the War of 1812. The people there suffered from discrimination by powerful white politicians in Halifax. The smelly dumps and factories, which Halifax didn't want, were encouraged to locate in Africville. Yet the city failed to provide important services such as water, streetlights or fire and police protection.

Portia taught the youngest children in Africville's two-roomed school. Sometimes it was chilly, even though there was a wood-stove. The warmest things in the room were the smiles of her pupils. Their teacher smiled back. The pupils thought Miss White was "awful nice".

AFRICVILLE

The white politicians did not listen to the people of Africville who tried to change things. The city tore down their houses and relocated them, often against their wishes. Africville was destroyed in the name of "urban renewal" between 1964 and 1969. The people had no choice but to move.

However, these people formed associations so that Africville would never be erased from their memories. In 2002, their efforts resulted in a plaque being erected by the National Historic Sites and Monuments Board of Canada to mark the historic significance of Africville.

Lessons No Matter What

THE DEPRESSION

During the economic crisis of the Depression in the 1930s, money was hard to come by. Reverend White and his musical children held benefit concerts at the Casino Theatre. The money earned was given to the church. William Andrew also saw that at a time of great unemployment, Black people were losing their jobs before white people did. He launched a Five-Year Programme to raise money to begin vocational schools within churches to train people for better jobs.

The young woman knew that she had one gift all her own—her wonderful singing voice. She had to give her creative side a chance to develop, or she would never escape her feelings of unhappiness.

Portia was paid only twenty cents an hour as a teacher. Singing lessons with Bertha Cruikshanks at the Halifax Conservatory of Music cost $3.50 an hour. Portia, however, was determined. After a long day at school, she would have to hurry to catch a train back to Halifax for her lessons, and she would do it no matter what the weather. "First you dream and then you lace up your walking-shoes!" she said.

She sang at every chance. Portia even became the director of the Cornwallis Street Baptist Church choir. Her eldest sister Helena played the organ.

Portia and friends around 1930

18

THE NOVA SCOTIA HOME FOR COLORED CHILDREN

When children were orphans, or if their parents could not look after them, orphanages might become their home. But Black children were sometimes turned away from these institutions. In 1921, crowds of white and Black citizens gathered in Dartmouth to celebrate the creation of the Nova Scotia Home for Colored Orphans, a place where orphans of African descent and others would be cared for and educated. Music was always an important part of the studies at the Home, and when Portia was twenty, she taught at the Home for one year. Her sister Yvonne was the music teacher there in the 1960s. Throughout the years, the students had a reputation for their musical talents. They often gave concerts and even radio broadcasts. One newspaper called them "Good Entertainers." In the 1940s, these singers attracted the attention of Dr. Helen Creighton, a famous Nova Scotian who collected folklore music. Creighton visited the Home to record their songs, noting she "enjoyed every minute of the afternoon" as the children sang their hearts out for her.

Trials and Triumphs

When she was twenty-three years old, Portia gave birth to a baby boy. She named him Gerald. As a young unmarried woman, she made the difficult decision to entrust the baby to her cousin to raise as her own son.

Portia's first "official" successes soon came her way. Portia won the Helen Campbell Kennedy Cup for her mezzo-soprano solos three times. A trophy is usually returned so it can be given to the next winner. Portia won the prize so many times that the beautiful silver cup was given to her to keep. "That gave me a boost," Portia said, and it made her all the more determined to become a professional singer.

The name Portia White was engraved on the Helen Campbell Kennedy Cup in 1935, 1937 and 1938. The year her name was not on the cup, a sad thing had happened—her father had become very ill.

Bill White

IZIE AND WILLIAM ANDREW'S CHILDREN SHINE AS ADULTS

The White children shone as adults. Helena became a secretary at Acadia University, where there is a scholarship named after her. Nettie worked as a supervisor with the federal Department of Health and Welfare. Mildred met members of the American branch of the White family when she moved to Ohio. George became a pharmacist, known for his "warm personality and thoughtfulness." Jack helped form the Canadian Negro Progress Club in 1952 and was politically active. Bill was the first Black Canadian to run in a federal election in 1949. He loved working with choirs and founded the Girls' and Boys' Glee Club in Agincourt, Ontario. He earned the Order of Canada in 1971 for "his contribution to better relations and understanding between people of different racial backgrounds."

The Family

On September 9, 1936, Izie answered the phone. Suddenly, her usually cheerful, smiling dark eyes filled with tears. Jack, Portia's younger brother, had never seen his mother cry. He knew at once that his father was dead.

Their father had been a very special person. William Andrew had become Dr. White shortly before his death, when Acadia University made him an honourary Doctor of Divinity. Dr. White had made many important contributions to the church and the community. Cornwallis St. Baptist Church was filled the day of his funeral. People lined up outside the doors and down the street. It was one of the largest funerals in Halifax.

Reverend White's son Jack remembered his father's great love for people—especially his children. Jack summed up his feelings simply— "he is the greatest individual I ever met."

All her life, Portia kept the ring that William Andrew had given her, a souvenir of World War One, it apparently had been nicked by an enemy bullet. Whenever she had a chance, Portia spoke of her father's achievements. She remembered his encouragement. It was sad that the man who always insisted his children do their best did not live to see their successes.

Jack, Portia, Bill in Toronto in 1952

It was a difficult time financially for the family without Reverend White's income. To help cover expenses, Portia's mother took in boarders, people who paid money to stay with them. Her brother, Bill, dropped out of university because he needed to work to help the family. Another brother stopped school for a time, even though he was only fourteen, so that he, too, might find a job.

A few years later, sadness again visited the Whites. The third youngest child, Evelyn, died at only twelve years of age after a terrible illness. Evelyn had a beautiful soprano voice, "just like the singers on the radio," her sister Yvonne and brother Lorne thought. It seemed unjust that her talent was stilled in October, 1939.

Please MARK and RETURN — HELP TO ELECT

Name:

Address:

Phone:

I WILL HELP THE NDP BY:

Putting Up A Sign

Making A Donation

Distributing Leaflets

Canvassing For Support

Working In Committee Rooms

Working At Home

Joining The Dovercourt NDP

Other

JACK WHITE

DOVERCOURT NDP — 531-3558

PRINTED BY WHITTEN LITHO.

Helena

Not Discouraged

MUSIC LOVERS IN HALIFAX

Halifax has a long history of loving music. The earliest musical society in all of British North America began in Halifax in 1769. More than a hundred years later, in 1906, the Halifax Ladies' Musical Club was created to promote music in the city.

These troubles seemed to push Portia's dreams of becoming a singer further away. She was now in her late twenties and, by this time, most classical music students were studying in Europe. The young woman didn't even know how she was going to pay for lessons at the Halifax Conservatory. Portia's family needed her more than ever.

But Portia was not ready to give up, and fortunately there were people who wanted to help.

The Halifax Ladies' Musical Club was a group of women who helped nurture music in the city. They put on concerts, brought special performers to Halifax and gave local students the chance to sing or play in productions. In 1939, the Halifax Ladies' Musical Club decided to do something exceptional. They thought Miss White had outstanding talent. They gave her a scholarship to pay for her singing lessons.

Portia gave a sigh of relief. Now, with help carrying her financial burden, she could work harder toward her dream of performing on stage. And she was going to have a new teacher.

Halifax Ladies' Musical Club

Changes 1939

WARTIME PERFORMERS

Lots of musical entertainment came to town during the war.

Three hundred entertainers were registered with the Concert Parties Division of the Halifax Citizens' Auxiliary War Services Committee.

The entertainers included: the YMCA Orpheus Male Choir; Scotia Singers; Halifax Conservatory Choir; Dalhousie Glee Club; the *Halifax Herald* and the *Halifax Mail* Harmonica Band; Betty Cobb and her dancing troupe; Muriel Mosher and a troupe of dancers; Prince Edward Island Highlanders Concert Party; 35th Battalion Halifax High School Cadets Fife and Drum Band; and the Happy Hoe-downers— to name a few. Portia was excited that so much "exceptional" talent had come to Halifax. One of her favourite entertainers was accordion player Dixie Dean.

Portia always thought positively. She believed "things just come my way." It seemed true in some way in 1939. Two important changes happened on the Halifax cultural scene which helped Portia's career.

The first event was the beginning of World War Two. War itself was not a good thing, but some good things happened because of the war. Wartime helped provide jobs for many entertainers. The port of Halifax was suddenly full of thousands of military people coming and going. They needed cheering up as they gathered from all across Canada, waiting to go to war. All sorts of people got a chance to perform for the troops. From dancers, to comedy acts, to bands and singers—Halifax was shimmering with entertainers. Portia was one of these performers.

THE WORLD AND CANADA, MUSICAL IMPORTANCE

The Halifax Conservatory of Music decided that they were fortunate to have Dr. Vinci as a teacher. Canada, at the time, was thought to be a "baby" in the world of classical music. In Europe, the roots went back for hundreds of years. Canadian students usually went to Europe to train. The Halifax Conservatory of Music was glad that they had an Italian expert right in the city.

Dr. Vinci worked at the Halifax Conservatory of Music until 1949, when he went to Banff, Alberta. He taught singing and directed operas there for twenty summers, until 1968. A building at the Banff Centre is named in his honour.

Portia's New Teacher

The arrival of a new music teacher was the second change in the Halifax cultural scene. The next person to help Portia's career was Ernesto Vinci from Italy. Dr. Vinci had studied both medicine and music. As a well-known baritone singer, Vinci had performed at the famous Italian opera house, La Scala. By 1938, Vinci and his wife disliked the politics in Italy so much that they moved to North America. He could not work as a doctor in Canada, but he was happy to teach music at the Halifax Conservatory of Music.

When Dr. Vinci first heard Portia's marvellous voice, he thought of a famous American singer. "How many Marian Andersons have you in North America?" he is reported to have asked. But the talented Portia had not yet sung a major concert. She was performing around Halifax—at teas, for soldiers and even making a few dollars singing with a jazz band for a local department store. There was a long way to go to make singing her living, and at almost thirty years of age she needed to get there quickly.

Dr. Ernesto Vinci

Halifax Conservatory of Music

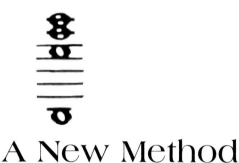

A New Method

MARIAN ANDERSON

Marian Anderson was an important American classical singer born in Philadelphia, Pennsylvania, in 1897. She trained in Europe, then earned worldwide respect despite widespread prejudice against Black people. In 1939, she was refused permission to sing inside a hall in Washington. Instead, she gave a famous concert outdoors at the Lincoln Memorial.

Starting her career a little later, Portia was often called "Canada's Marian Anderson." Both women sang in the same range, began singing with choirs and had financial support from the community. But Portia tired of the comparisons. She thought their individual life experiences helped them translate songs differently. Portia said the fact that both stars were Black women was just a coincidence, as if they had been "born on the same block."

Dr. Vinci taught Portia a way of singing called *bel canto,* or "beautiful song" in Italian. First, Vinci placed his student's voice. Portia had sung as a mezzo-soprano. But she learned that "my voice belonged naturally in the contralto register." From then on, Portia sang at a lower pitch.

Portia studied breath control, "...the basis for the agility and stamina needed by a singer." Singers needed to be able to sing as many as twenty songs at a recital.

The student learned that "coordination and poise are also important in developing this style." Fortunately, Portia had a good deal of natural poise that people commented on all of her life. Standing at five feet eight inches, she had a graceful, regal presence.

She learned opera arias, folk songs and spirituals in English, Spanish, French and German. Portia's talent with languages at school certainly came to her aid now. Each time the student sang, she had to think about breathing, diction (how to make the words sound), phrasing (how groups of words fit together), and following the music—in addition to remembering the right words in another language.

Hard Work

THE WHITES PERFORM FOR THE TROOPS IN DIFFERENT WAYS

June, Evelyn, Jack and Yvonne, known as the White Quartet, performed lively songs such as "The Pie Song" for the troops. Portia took part in classical concerts, singing in more than two shows a night at the YMCA Hostel or the Knights of Columbus Hall. Once, she and seven other of Dr. Vinci's students gave a program in French to an enthusiastic audience. The singer felt honoured to perform for people from many different backgrounds. She explained that the soldiers were "...genuinely appreciative of good music and I have sung them operatic numbers as well as others." When some servicemen gave her a silver pin to thank her, Portia was "tremendously touched."

The lessons could be difficult. Students had to stand in uncomfortable positions so that they could sing better. Dr. Vinci poked them below their ribs to make them feel their breath coming from their diaphragm. He wanted his students to work harder all the time. Sometimes Vinci thought that Portia didn't work hard enough. Portia always loved fun, but she admitted that she needed someone to give her "a push."

Vinci pushed her, but he had many good things to say about his pupil. "She is a genius at feeling," Vinci enthused. This helped her understand the poetry in her music, "because great songs have great poems." He warned that Portia "will have to study the language and the culture of the songs she sings, so that she can interpret them to others." The teacher felt that his special pupil had "one of the most beautiful contralto voices there are. With work and experience she can be of the first class."

The teacher wanted his student to practise, practise, practise.

The YMCA in Halifax

A CITY CALLED HEAVEN

On April 19, 1940, Portia took part in the first radio broadcast from the YMCA Hostel. The song she sang was "A City Called Heaven". Her rich voice came over the airwaves with the words of the traditional spiritual, which must have comforted many listeners:

I am a poor pilgrim of sorrow
I've come to this great land alone
I've heard of a city called heaven
I've heard of a city called heaven
I've started to make heaven my home.

Halifax Star

The result of Portia's performances using the *bel canto* method was that people were even more impressed with her talent. At a concert to help the Red Cross, she won lots of applause for her music, "her poise and charming simplicity". A reviewer praised her voice as being "its finest, rich and pure with strength and volume in its low range and bell-like clarity in the high notes". The writer predicted that if the young singer continued to improve at her present rate, "Portia White will bring international fame to Halifax one day."

In May 1940, one of Dr. Vinci's students, Shirley Blois, had the lead in a benefit concert for the Save the Children Fund. However, several days before, Blois became ill and cancelled. Portia stepped in. She sang a group of three spirituals. Spirituals began as songs sung by Black slaves. By Portia's day, they had changed and become songs delivered in a more formal, classical style, mostly by Black American artists. The audience "particularly enjoyed" Portia's spirituals. She was becoming the darling of Halifax.

EDITH READ

Edith Read was born in 1879. She earned a Master's degree in mathematics and received an Honourary Doctor of Laws from Dalhousie University. Until her death in 1963, she had a reputation for helping people. When over a thousand children were evacuated from Britain and arrived in Toronto, Read gave up her summer vacation in 1940 to help find homes for them. The one hundred War Guests who attended Branksome Hall appreciated Read's assistance as they adjusted to their new life. They had many things to discover in Canada—from hotdogs to mosquitos.

Enter Edith Read

In August 1941, one person's summer vacation changed Portia's life. Miss Edith Read travelled from Toronto back to her home province of Nova Scotia for a holiday. Read had a doctorate degree and a job as principal of a private girl's school in Toronto, Branksome Hall.

Read knew a talented musician when she heard one. After hearing Portia sing at a tea, Read asked herself, "Why isn't the young woman on a bigger stage?" Read wasn't one for sitting on a good idea about how to help someone. She took action to get Portia's voice heard before a wider audience. Read received the backing of the Branksome Hall Alumnae Association and arranged a concert at the Eaton Auditorium on November 7, 1941. Portia was going to Toronto.

Edith Read

28

A thoughtful Portia

PORTIA SCORES A TRIUMPH

An important music critic, Hector Charlesworth, had wonderful things to say about Portia's concert in Toronto. Under the headline "Young Coloured Singer Scored Authentic Triumph Here," the *Globe and Mail* writer said: "Given backing and opportunity she would go as far as Marian Anderson."

To Toronto

Before the fall of 1941, Portia had only sung at four large concerts. These all took place in the Maritimes—two in Halifax; one at Mount Allison University in Sackville, New Brunswick; and one at Acadia University in Wolfville, Nova Scotia. It was hard to believe that she was making her professional debut in Toronto, one of Canada's largest cities.

If she thought about it too much, her stomach felt quivery from the "butterflies" that fluttered inside. However, Portia was able to trick herself. She decided to pretend that she was at a dress rehearsal, and the seats were empty.

As she had been taught, she took her place grandly on stage and waited for her piano accompanist to reach the right spot in the music. She took a deep breath, opened her mouth and sang.

But Portia wasn't dreaming or imagining. The people were there, and they loved Portia's singing. Portia's brown eyes sparkled with happiness when they clapped and clapped. She knew the concert was a success.

A Professional Singer

The same day as the Toronto concert, Portia signed a contract. A branch of the Oxford University Press which arranged concerts for Canadian performers wanted to represent her. Portia was breathless with excitement. It's "all too wonderful. I cannot yet believe it is true," she told the reporters.

Things happened very quickly for Portia. With the magic came some important and scary decisions. Portia decided she needed to devote herself entirely to studying music. She could not have two full-time jobs, so she telegrammed her resignation as a teacher at the Africville school. She was now truly on the path to becoming a professional singer.

The next step was for Portia to boost her fame in and outside of Canada. But how to take her career in this direction? Edith Read had more surprises. Read knew the general manager of the famous Metropolitan Opera in New York. The young singer was very glad for Read's continuing support. "She came to me out of a blue sky," Portia marvelled, "and has been with me ever since."

A portrait of Portia by Hedley G. Rainnie

Edward Johnson made up as Rodolfo for the opera *La Bohème*

EDWARD JOHNSON

Edward Johnson was born in Guelph, Ontario in 1878. Like Portia, he began his career singing in choirs. Then, called Edoardo de Giovanni, he became a famous tenor in Italy and South America. He joined the Metropolitan Opera in New York in 1922. He worked there as manager from 1935 until 1950. During this time, "the Met" would not hire Black performers to play with white singers.

Johnson kindly gave advice to the little-known Miss White. Some time later, he put a concert program of Portia in one of his scrapbooks, albums filled mostly with photos of white stars. Johnson helped many musicians and donated money to schools in Guelph, so that music could be taught. A school there has been named to honour this important Canadian and the Faculty of Music building at the University of Toronto is also named for him.

Edward Johnson's Advice

The man Edith Read knew, Edward Johnson, was a very important person internationally in music. He thought that Portia should make an appearance in New York to introduce her to the world. The Town Hall was the wonderful venue where American singers, soprano Dorothy Maynard and contralto Marian Anderson, had their debuts. Portia would be the first Canadian invited to sing there. But Johnson recommended that Portia spend time studying with Dr. Vinci, travelling and giving concerts. He thought she needed to build up her experience before going to the United States. Portia followed his advice.

In 1943, Portia was required to have throat surgery to correct damage left from "strep". Except for a short time off to recover, Portia spent the next few years travelling across Canada. She gave concerts in many parts of the Maritimes: Moncton, Fredericton, Saint John, Truro, Liverpool and Acadia. Her reputation grew as she performed in Victoria and Vancouver, British Columbia; Edmonton and Calgary, Alberta; Regina and Saskatoon, Saskatchewan; Winnipeg, Manitoba; Port Arthur (now Thunder Bay), Ontario; and Montreal, Quebec. She also gave a command performance in Ottawa for the Governor General.

Marian Anderson

PORTIA AND SPIRITUALS

Spirituals was the name given to songs which were first sung by slaves from Africa. Two singers Portia admired, Marian Anderson and Roland Hayes, helped make them very well-known. Soon, audiences almost expected to hear Black artists sing spirituals. Early in her career, Portia said that as solos they were not part of her Nova Scotian heritage and she wanted to study them more. She may later have decided to accept the challenge to celebrate this kind of music, and spirituals were soon the favourites of many of her fans.

Canada loves Portia

As Portia travelled across Canada, all the cities which had only been dots in the atlas were now places where people were paying to hear her sing. Portia sang the crowds' favourite songs, from German opera arias to old English pieces. She charmed Acadians and Quebecers with numbers in French. She sang the spirituals, the songs of sorrow and hope for Black slaves in the United States and which continued to express the feelings people shared about the ongoing war.

Portia noted the special effect she had on the audience. When she sang before 1,400 people at St. John, New Brunswick, she wrote to Dr. Vinci, "One man fainted during my singing of 'The Lord is My Light', and most of the congregation wept during 'Were You There?' I must confess that it gave me an unusual sense of power to see the handkerchiefs appearing in all directions."

As the day approached for her New York debut, Portia had done a lot of singing in the short time since her first Toronto appearance, but was it enough?

THE TOWN HALL

123 WEST 43rd STREET, NEW YORK, N. Y.

PORTIA WHITE

ALFRED SCOTT · PUBLISHER · 156 FIFTH AVENUE, NEW YORK

A LETTER OF SUPPORT

A letter from B.A. Husbands, President of the Colored Citizens Improvement League in Halifax, spoke about the help Dr. Vinci and the Halifax Ladies' Musical Club had given Portia. It also said:

It is with profound gratitude and pleasure that the coloured citizens of this city and province note the acclaim accorded Miss Portia White from the whole Dominion of Canada because of her outstanding contralto voice and her ability as a concert artist.

Her many friends and admirers throughout the city and province will eagerly await further successes following her New York performance.

Support for New York

Then came the big day, a day which could make or break her future. If she performed well at the Town Hall concert, an international career might come quickly. But Portia and Dr. Vinci had chosen many difficult numbers. Her teacher wanted the critics to see that his pupil was a mature and gifted star. Vinci wasn't worried. If the critics didn't like the performance, her international career would simply be "delayed a little".

The Saturday night before the New York event, Portia was so nervous she couldn't sleep. She lay in bed, going over the program again and again. Not wanting to make any mistakes, she excitedly let herself do the whole show in her mind "complete with encores."

Portia knew that she had a lot of support. The mayor of Halifax, John E. Lloyd, sent her flowers from the people in her home city. A very proud letter was printed in the Halifax paper from the Black community.

But as she prepared to go to the concert, Vinci could not be found. Portia did not want to leave without her teacher. But she also did not want to be late for her debut. After postponing the decision as long as possible, Portia sped to Town Hall.

Town Hall
March 13, 1944

FLAGS

The American Stars and Stripes was adopted as the flag of the United States by Congress in 1777. Canada's current flag, the red and white maple leaf, did not become official until February 15, 1965. In Portia's day, contests were being held to decide on a new flag, but it was complicated to have everyone agree on what best represented Canada. The flag that was in use from 1924 to 1965 was called the Canadian Red Ensign. It had the Union Jack on the top left corner and the Canadian Coat of Arms on a shield on the right side. The background was a bright red. This colourful Canadian Red Ensign and the bright American Stars and Stripes would have made cheery decorations on Portia's grand evening at Town Hall.

Portia arrived at Town Hall and was relieved to find Dr. Vinci there. But she was very nearly late. There was not a second to spare and no time to feel nervous. Almost as soon as she got there, Portia had to go on stage.

More than one thousand people sat in the red plush seats of the hall. A newspaper explained that they had come because "the grapevine gossip of the music world reported that something special was going to happen..." People of all descriptions and ethnic backgrounds came to hear if the stories of Miss White's vocal magic were true. Some were friends from Nova Scotia, others were people Edith Read knew, and many were simply music lovers.

The Canadian Counsel, Canada's representative to the United States, sat in a special box of seats. It had been draped with the red ensign for Canada. One writer noted that flags for both Canada and the United States "waved gloriously from the balcony arch, symbolic of the fellowship of these two countries: symbolic of their belief in human achievement, black and white."

"Destined for world fame"

"She can thrill her listeners to the marrow"

IN PRAISE OF PORTIA

The New York Post reviewer said: The Halifaxians have made no mistake in getting behind Miss White, because while she is a great singer in the making rather than a finished artist, she has big potentials..." She "has in addition three-important P's: poise, personality and punch—but a nice kind of intelligent punch. There's a gleam in her eye which is infectious, but her exuberance is preceded by thinking which is well schooled and emanates from a brain which apparently clicks..."

When Portia opened her mouth, the music poured out. She sang, among other songs, "Là-bas sur les montagnes" in French; "Der Freund" in German; and "Think on Me" in English. She became so much a part of each note that she was "transported, lifted so completely" out of her body. When the music ended, she felt emptied, "like a vessel that's been thoroughly drained."

The outpouring of song left the audience in awe. They called Portia back on stage again and again, for three ovations. Everyone knew they had witnessed a marvellous event.

Reviewers found many ways to praise Portia. The *New York Times* compared her to Marian Anderson in an article with the headline "An Unheralded Star is Born."

Her international debut was a success. Portia signed a contract with Columbia Concerts, one of the biggest agencies representing international stars. Their brochures trumpeted: "Portia White, Contralto. A Young Artist Who is Destined for World Fame." It seemed that nothing could go wrong.

♪♪ Money and Stardom

THE PORTIA WHITE PRIZE

The Portia White Fund was created by two governments in 1944: the city of Halifax and the province of Nova Scotia. In 1949, the province committed itself to supporting other talented young artists and performers through the Nova Scotia Talent Trust. In 1995, the Portia White Prize was established by the province so that writers, photographers, pianists, actors and other singers could have help with their careers. Dr. George Elliot Clarke, a writer and grandson of Portia's sister, Nettie, received the prize in 1998. Sylvia Hamilton, who made the impressive film about Portia titled *Think on Me*, was awarded the prize in 2002 for her work as a filmmaker. Both are respected as cultural leaders and mentors to young people.

Her career was going well, but Portia had huge costs to cover. Out of their fees, artists had to pay a percentage for their manager, accompanist, travelling costs and clothes. The expensive gowns she wore were important. Before she opened her mouth to sing, reviewers noted if she had on a pale green gown or a black lace one. Portia paid a great deal of money for the lovely costumes made by a woman in Toronto. The star found that her expenses were enormous.

Portia also believed that good things came to her out of "the clear sky." A fund to help Portia's career was created by the municipal government of the city of Halifax and the provincial government of the province of Nova Scotia. The Portia White Fund marked the first time that two levels of Canadian government joined to help an artist's career. The province and the city wanted Portia to become an international star and bring fame to Halifax and Nova Scotia. At the award presentation in May, 1944, they also gave Portia a white fox cape to wear to receptions after her concerts.

Living in New York

In the mid 1940s, Portia moved to New York. Here, she lived closer to her managers and enjoyed being in the centre of the North American music world. She went to concerts whenever she could "get tickets." Portia was "thrilled" when she saw *Porgy and Bess*, one of the first all-Black operas. She said in an interview that she was stirred to see a "vast attendance" at Madison Square Gardens "for an opera presented by members of her own race."

Portia was a stylish young woman, very cosmopolitan, smartly dressed and carrying a briefcase full of music and dashing here and there. In a letter to Mrs. Vinci, Portia wrote "New York is very exciting. I have walked for miles every day just window shopping." Indeed, New York was a grand city to live in with many opportunities, but Portia missed the closeness of her family. She often stayed with a family, explaining "that's the nearest thing to home."

WOMEN'S FASHION

When Portia lived in New York, she loved looking at new clothes. "The stores on Fifth Avenue are just what one needs in depressed moments" she exclaimed. While the costumes she wore at her evening concerts were spectacular, Portia always appeared well-dressed in her daily life. She looked like a very modern young woman wearing high-heeled shoes, a dress or skirt that went to the knee, and usually a hat.

Women's fashions changed a lot during Portia's life. When she was born, women's dresses were quite long. In Portia's late adulthood, it became acceptable for women to reveal their legs in miniskirts.

Portia Unwinds

When she wasn't working, the star had simple ways to relax. Sometimes she sat quietly doing needlework or crocheting, "making things with my hands for people I like."

The kitchen was another place where Portia could be creative, even though wartime rationing meant she had to use less butter and sugar. Spaghetti, lemon cakes and Nova Scotia salmon were some of the dishes Portia cooked. Her mother said her daughter made a "good pan of biscuits". Sometimes the results in the kitchen were not so successful. Once she served a very undercooked chicken to her brother Jack and his wife, Alma. Everyone laughed. Another time when she was cooking, she "spilled something and slipped on it" and broke her toe.

She liked to go to the movies, and she still loved reading. Fantasy or books on "imaginative subjects" interested her. Like her father, who was an able amateur psychologist, Portia enjoyed psychology. "Psychology," Portia said, "has its value to a concert singer as well as a preacher." It was important to know about feelings and motivations in both professions.

LIKES AND DISLIKES

Portia had her own distinctive likes and dislikes. Her favourite meal before a concert was a huge steak. She hated reptiles. She joked that the fashion accessory she liked best was a handbag with money in it. She had many friends and especially enjoyed people who had "the courage to be naturall'. She preferred Christopher Marlowe to Shakespeare, but Shakespeare had written her favourite play, *The Merchant of Venice,* as it had "named" her. Marian Anderson was her favourite contralto singer and Wagner her favourite composer. When it came to orchestras, she favoured Bernard Naylor's Little Symphony, which the British composer and conductor founded in Montreal in 1942.

In Love with Music

NATHANIEL DETT

Composers, such as Henry Thacker Burleigh and Nathaniel Dett changed simple slave songs into arrangements for recital singers. Nathaniel Dett was born in Niagara Falls, Ontario in 1882. He became very well-known, especially in the United States, for his work as a composer, teacher and choir conductor. He was interested in celebrating Black music and collected spirituals and folk songs. Dett died in 1943. Today the Nathaniel Dett Chorale, Canada's first professional choral group dedicated to Afrocentric music of all styles, bears his name. It was founded in 1998 by Brainerd Blyden-Taylor, who came from Trinidad to Canada and led some wonderful choirs. Dett would love the way the young people of the Nathaniel Dett Chorale interpret his music today.

Of course, Portia was never far from music. Her mother reported she liked "listening to hillbilly music on the radio, if you can believe it." Portia adored classical music, but she didn't mind some popular music of the time. She admired George Gershwin, who had composed *Porgy and Bess*, and Spike Jones, who created very funny songs with silly noises and sound effects like gun shots. Whenever she was at her mother's house, Portia, like other members of the family, would always be singing. And of course, in Halifax, Dr. Vinci was nearby to prod her into working whenever he could. The singer's brother, Lorne, says that Portia couldn't be in the front room rehearsing without "all of Belle Aire Terrace knowing what was going on. She had a big voice..." Lorne recalls, "...rehearsals were kind of earth shattering." The sadness from her childhood days was gone. Now Portia knew she could sing all she wanted and, as the large numbers of people at her concerts proved, the world would listen.

YVONNE WHITE

Yvonne is another White who is brimming with musical talent. She worked as a music teacher with orphans at the Nova Scotia Home for Colored Children. She has performed many places, often singing classical pieces like her sister Portia, as well as gospel numbers. Yvonne's voice has brought pleasure to many people. She has helped raise money for causes such as rebuilding an historic church at Lunenburg, Nova Scotia, which was destroyed in a fire in 1993.

Yvonne White in 1982

Visits Home

Portia missed her friends and family while touring and living away. She was always excited to go back for a visit. She went to concerts of her brothers' jazz band. She played tennis and bridge with her brothers and sisters. After grace was said at mealtime, they chattered non-stop.

Her younger sister Yvonne remembers "It was always a joyous occasion" when Portia came home. One rainy day, Yvonne was driving Portia when her elder sister decided they had to stop in Canning. A Mr. Eaton lived there, who had developed a Portia apple. It is a red McIntosh which "tastes very nice," according to Yvonne. However, Portia didn't know where the right person lived, and there were many Eatons. "You can guess who had to knock at the door!" Yvonne laughs. "I was soaked!"

"Finally, we found Mr. Ernest Eaton, and then I had to slosh out to the orchard to see these trees! Portia wouldn't leave until she had two boxes of apples to ship to her friends and some hampers to take with us!"

LORNE'S CAREER

Some time later, Portia told Lorne that she would like to give him a voice lesson. "You have a big voice. I'm sorry that I haven't been around to do more. But this is what I would like to do for you."

Lorne says "I only had that one lesson, and it was the only lesson I ever had." But Lorne felt it made a big difference. Lorne had a happy career in music which included fourteen seasons on a television show with Anne Murray called *Singalong Jubilee*.

Dr. Lorne White

Loving Sister

Portia's youngest and perhaps favourite bother was Lorne. He explains that his sister "always knew where I was." Once, in 1944, Lorne and a fellow Air Cadet were on a train which stopped in Moncton, New Brunswick. Lorne was surprised when Portia stepped aboard. "I'm going to take you boys for dinner," she said. "You can take the next train back to Halifax."

She asked them what their plans were since they had finished high school. "I'll get a job as a [train] porter," Lorne affirmed. He thought that was where he could make the most money, as there were so few jobs open to Blacks.

"I just gave a concert," Portia replied, "and I know there is a small bursary available. If you write to the president of Acadia, you might be able to go there." Lorne did go to Acadia University. With the bursary and the money he earned at different jobs, he was able to finish two degrees.

He is grateful for Portia's love and special interest, which greatly influenced his career. "Portia was always there," Lorne concludes lovingly.

THE BEAT GOES ON

The music "gene" strongly continues in the White family. Lorne and Mary's daughters, Holly, Shelly and Lee are gospel singers. Chris, Bill and Vivian's son, is the artistic director of the Ottawa Folk Festival. He is also a singer and composer of songs which make kids howl with laughter. Chris and his sister Laurie accomplished something that Portia could not. They collected recordings of their aunt's live concerts which were held at the National Library of Canada. From these they produced a CD for the general public. *First You Dream* is available in libraries or through www.cdwhite.com.

Aunt Portia

Portia was a kind aunt. She always had a smile, joke or a sweet for her nephews and nieces. One nephew, Don Oliver, grew up to be the first Black man appointed to the Canadian Senate. As a little boy, he remembers how his Aunt Portia impressed him. His mother was Helena, Portia's older sister. One night, Portia and other friends came over to visit at their house in Wolfville, Nova Scotia. The kids were supposed to be in bed, but they lay at the top of the stairs listening.

Don recalls on his website that his mother played Chopin on the piano: "Suddenly, when she finished, our tiny house was filled with an awesome, powerful contralto voice singing 'Think on Me.' Aunt Portia White was singing to my parents and some of their close friends. Portia's voice was so powerful and so beautiful that it not only filled our entire house but (as a twelve-year-old) I felt the house was shaking with its power and charm. I knew, at that young age, that I was in the presence of greatness."

FIRST YOU DREAM

PORTIA WHITE

THE ONLY ONE

Portia is often the only person of African descent in the groups posing for newspaper and concert photographs. It must have been an odd and lonely feeling. At the same time, Portia may have realized that her being among these performers and officials meant that other Canadian performers of African descent would be able to take their turn on the stage. Modern opera star Measha Brueggergosman also grew up in the Maritimes, in New Brunswick. She did not learn about Portia in school, but came to have a unique view of her. As a teenager, Measha played Portia in a movie.

Measha Brueggergosman as a teen

Feeling Unwelcome

Even in her home province, sometimes Portia was made to feel as if she didn't belong. The singer gave a concert under the dazzling chandeliers of the Lord Nelson Hotel's ballroom in Halifax, but this hotel, others in Halifax, and those in many cities did not allow Black people to stay there.

One manager showed Portia her room at a fancy hotel in a large Canadian city. He stated that she would "be expected not to appear in the main dining room." Calmly, Portia pointed out that it was "very strange that someone sponsored by a government of Canada should not be acceptable." Upset, the man sped away, although he later returned. He told the star that she would be welcome in the dining room. "Thank you very much," Portia answered, "but I always prefer to eat in my own room."

Portia had a desire to sing opera. However, in North America until the 1950s, there were operas for Black performers and different operas for whites. A chance for Portia to sing in a Black opera fell through, and there were not many other opportunities.

A Sad Story

Portia's hairdresser was Viola Desmond, a woman who had a sad experience with racial inequality.

It wasn't always easy to fit Miss White in for a hair appointment. The star had a full schedule, and so did Desmond. Desmond ran her own hairdressing business and a "beauty school," a place where girls learned to become beauticians or estheticians.

When Desmond's car broke down on the evening of November 8, 1944, in New Glasgow, Nova Scotia, she decided to relax and take in a movie while waiting for the repairs. The ticket seller at the Roseland Theatre refused to sell her a place downstairs. She gave her a ticket for the upstairs balcony where Black people were supposed to sit. In many parts of North America, Black people were not welcome to sit where they wanted in buses, restaurants or movie theatres.

Desmond did not see very well, so she calmly took a seat downstairs anyway.

The ticket seller and then the theatre manager told her to move. Desmond politely refused, and the police were called. A police officer and the theatre manager seized Desmond, carried her outside and put her into a cab which drove her to the police station. She spent the night locked in a cell, full of male prisoners. Desmond was the only woman. She sat awake all night, with her gloves on.

In the morning, a judge fined Desmond twenty dollars and ordered her to spend thirty days in jail. The charge was defrauding or cheating the government because she had not payed the one-cent amusement tax on the higher-priced downstairs seats. It did not matter that Desmond had tried to pay.

Desmond was helped by members of the Halifax Black community, Dr. and Mrs. Oliver, and through the newly created Nova Scotia Association for the Advancement of Coloured People (NSAACP). They fought a legal battle which freed Desmond from the charges because of a "technicality".

Such was the day-to-day life faced by some Black Canadians in Nova Scotia in the 1940s. Demeaning social customs and prejudice were and still are hard to change.

The United States

Portia visited many parts of the United States, where she felt racism was worse than in Canada.

"I was very depressed when I first came to the United States by the evidences of segregation and discrimination," she said. In *Ebony*, a magazine created in 1942 featuring Black Americans, Portia expressed amazement at the segregation in the American army. She bragged that her two brothers in the Canadian Army were "treated as equals of all other members of the armed forces. My father was the only Negro chaplain in the British Forces during the First World War," Portia told the reporter. "The colour problem as it exists in the United States is not known in Nova Scotia," she explained. "While coloured people have established their own churches in Nova Scotia, there is no other society distinction made and even the so-called 'coloured' churches have mixed congregations."

She concluded: "I feel a greater unity with coloured people everywhere as a result of my stay in the U.S. And I am immensely proud of the advance we are making in spite of the efforts of those who would deny us equality."

OSCAR PETERSON VISITS THE AMERICAN SOUTH

Racism was especially terrible in the southern United States, where most of the slaves and slave owners had lived. The scars of this time were still ugly, and Portia was "astounded" by how bad conditions were in this area for people of African descent (then called "colored" or "Negro").

A few years later, in 1950, Canadian jazz pianist Oscar Peterson became very upset when he went to the south to play. His fellow white musicians were given nice hotel rooms in a good section of town. Peterson had to stay in very rundown places. Things had not changed from the times when Portia had visited this part of the United States.

More Concerts

TWO INJURED AIRMEN

Two injured airmen, one from eastern and the other from western Canada, came together while recovering in Toronto. Clifton Outhouse and Lew Watt shared an interest in music. They created a song called "Waiting For You", and a nurse wrote down the notes. The song was about how hard it is to be away from those you love during the war. An officer took the two soldiers and their music to the Maple Leaf Gardens Victory Rally. There they met a "beautiful, very dignified lady," the internationally famous Miss White. The men were thrilled when Portia agreed to sing their song in the concert—with them sitting on the stage and six thousand people listening.

Portia continued concertizing across Canada and the United States. She had support from the Halifax and Nova Scotian governments; church and women's groups and Black organizations. When she appeared for the second time in 1944 at New York's Town Hall it was under the sponsorship of the National Council of Negro Women. In Detroit, Missouri and Chicago, Portia was one of the many talented performers at the Negro Musical Festival which entertained thousands of people. In June 1944, Portia was back in Toronto and part of a huge United Nations Rally For Victory in Maple Leaf Gardens. Wherever the concert and whoever was in the audience, the famed singer rarely left the stage without a standing ovation.

Maple Leaf Gardens in Toronto

Exciting Honours

KARSH

Yousuf Karsh was a famous photographer who was born in Armenia in 1908, but escaped from the Turkish atrocities there with his family to Syria. As a young man, he was invited by his uncle to come to Canada. At sixteen, Karsh left most of his family and arrived on the ocean liner *Versailles*, on New Year's Eve, 1924 at Halifax Harbour. He never forgot the sound of the tinkling sleigh bells as he and his uncle George made their way through the city. As an adult, Karsh lived in Ottawa and Boston until his death in 2002. He earned a reputation around the globe with his photographs of over 15,000 people, among them notables such as politician, Sir Winston Churchill, and the artist, Georgia O'Keeffe. He also photographed some of Portia's favourites, singers Marian Anderson and Paul Robeson.

The world could not get enough of Portia. When the war ended, she participated in a film, *This is Canada*, which was made for the countries of the newly created United Nations. The film featured the Winnipeg ballet and the Canadian-Ukrainian Chorus. Portia sang her famous versions of "To the Queen of Heaven," "Cou-cou," and "Swing Low, Sweet Chariot."

Canadian artists Grant MacDonald, Hedley Rainnie and sculptor Harold Pfeiffer created her likeness. Karsh, the famous Canadian portrait photographer, took her picture. Singers need pictures for publicity material, but Karsh was expensive. However, he liked Portia. He felt that "undoubtedly she was living on a shoestring", and he did not charge as much as he usually did. Karsh found Portia had a "beautiful voice, glorious eyes, a sweet personality, and all the sincerity in the world. That day," he said, "I gave of my best and took untold pains."

The Life of a Star

A sketch of Portia by Murray Bonnycastle

One man, Murray Bonnycastle, who fell in love with Portia, wrote poems about her. Portia's sister-in-law, Vivian, describes some of the poems Bonnycastle wrote as "quite lovely." Their relationship ended, and Portia, in fact, never married. Perhaps being on the road so much made it difficult for the star to have a long-term relationship which could lead to marriage. Portia, however, enjoyed her life of travelling. "It does something to the imagination," she said.

Portia's life at this time was spent in hotels, travelling from city to city. Her singing had taken her across the United States and Canada, and now it was time to visit more of the world. In 1946, she went on a huge three-month tour of the West Indies, Latin and South America. Some of the costs for the trip were paid by several Halifax organizations of people of African descent.

Portia in Medellin, Columbia

RADIO

Radio developed quickly from 1894, when Guglielmo Marconi began tinkering with his spark transmitter in Bologna, Italy. In the book, *Radio's First Voice,* author Ormond Raby tells the story of the first voice broadcast by Canadian-born radio pioneer Reginald Fessenden in 1906. On Christmas Eve, Fessenden's wife and friend sang Christmas carols that were picked up by radio-equipped ships. When the first radio stations began in Nova Scotia, CHNS Halifax (1926) and CJCB Sydney (1928) only had programs of hockey, news and music a few hours a day. In 1936, the Canadian Radio Act created the Canadian Broadcasting Corporation, a national system of radio stations. Radio broadcasts were an important way for music stars to reach their fans. However, Portia once admitted to Dr. Vinci that although broadcasts could be thrilling, microphones frightened her. As a recital singer, Portia was used to performing without one.

The Caribbean, Central and South America

Portia toured the islands of Curaçao, Trinidad, Grenada, Jamaica, Barbados and several other countries. She enjoyed meeting people and experiencing other ways of life. One thing she found different was radio. North American radio broadcasts had no seconds to spare. In Bogota, the capitol of Columbia, they told her not to worry if the show ran over time. The interview went on ten minutes longer than scheduled, but nobody minded. People excitedly kept coming into the studio and taking the microphone to talk to Miss White. It was a new and casual approach.

Portia liked travelling, but this tour was very hectic. One night she performed in one country, and the next morning she would catch a plane to another country to give more concerts. Canadian opera star Emma Albani had always made sure that she arrived the day before a performance and had time to rest. Portia had little rest between concerts, and it was tiring for her voice. The tour, she felt, was a crazy whirlwind mixture of dream and nightmare.

A Special Fan

Walter Scott

A huge music fan, Walter Scott thinks he is a lucky man. He saw one of his favourite singers many times and in many different cities—even in Panama. When he was in his late teens, Walter took in one of Portia's early concerts in Amherst, Nova Scotia. Portia's cousin, Ronnie White, had told him about the event. It seemed as if almost all of Amherst's one thousand people were in the church. Portia delighted the full house, and Walter especially. He said "she had a gracious way, almost regal, with her head back. She also had expressive hands... I knew that we were in for a treat—and we were."

When he moved to Halifax, Walter would see Portia more often. She was always friendly and stopped to talk with him. Walter was in the navy and was going to miss one of Portia's concerts. "Come around to rehearsal some time," she said when she found out. So, before he had to sail, Walter saw Portia working with Dr. Vinci. "He was like a father to her," Walter explained.

During the war, a ship he was on landed in Panama, and Walter set out to visit the city. "It was quite surprising," Walter recounts, "that

MORE OF PORTIA AND WALTER'S STORY

In 1966, Walter's church in Toronto was having a special ceremony to celebrate a new addition. Portia came to sing. She lent Walter the lovely book of spirituals the Panamanians had given her so he could use it to prepare the concert program.

When he heard her sing at the church, Walter said Portia was as good as ever and "where she had left off in the forties." When Portia sang "Bless this House", everyone was excited. They gave Portia a huge bouquet of roses. The picture that Walter's friend, Angus Miller, took shows how happy and beautiful Portia was that evening (the photo is on page 58).

one of the first things I saw was a concert poster." On the poster was a familiar face— Portia was giving a concert that night. Excitedly, Walter called the theatre and was able to visit with the star for half an hour. He got to see part of the concert but was sad when he could not see it all. The Panama concert was very special. Portia was given a book of spirituals and a gold medal made by the Isthmian Negro Youth Congress for "distinguished cultural service and the promotion of better human relations."

Portia in Curacao in 1946

Portia and Gordon Kushner in Kingston, Jamaica, 1946

GORDON KUSHNER

Gordon Kushner was Portia's piano accompanist on many of her tours. He was born in Winnipeg in 1916 and had a very distinguished career as a teacher, music director and composer. He spent many years with the CBC and the Royal Conservatory of Music in Toronto after stints in the navy and on radio in Winnipeg. He said that when he first heard Portia sing, he almost fainted.

Time to Change

The tour of 1946 was Portia's last big tour. Even though she had only been singing professionally for five years, she knew she had some big problems. She realized that her voice had not had enough time for proper training. "Everything happened too fast to me. In Europe, singers study 10 or 12 years. I came up like a mushroom. I had studied only one year when I made [my] debut. Then a couple of years later the South American tour. After a while I found that I wasn't singing well."

Over the next few years, Portia's health began to decline, although she didn't like to talk about it or give many details. For several reasons, her career began to unravel. Critics complained of flaws in her voice, and the star herself said she was tired. She was also fed up with her management. She felt they could have handled her career better, given her more concerts with better money. Portia exclaimed that one letter from a manager "took away my breath." Another time she wanted to throw "the contract overboard."

Also, the letters which flew between Dr. Vinci, Edith Read and Portia's personal friend, Ruth Wilson, were full of accusations. Each

RUTH WILSON AND HEALTH CARE

Free hospital care began in Saskatchewan in 1947, when Premier Tommy Douglas brought in the first provincial hospital insurance program in Canada. However, it was not until 1966 that Parliament passed an act to support medical care in all the provinces. Portia's friend, Ruth Cook Wilson, knew how hard it was for families to pay their hospital bills. She was part of management at the Moncton Hospital, New Brunswick; a member of the American College of Hospital Administrators; and executive director of the Maritime Hospital Association (as the first woman in North America to hold this sort of post).

Ruth was born in New Jersey in 1895, and was inducted into the New Brunswick Business Hall of Fame after her death. During her life, she earned a certificate in aeronautical engineering and a pilot's licence (although she never drove a car). She was awarded an honourary Doctorate of Laws from St. Francis Xavier University in 1958 for her outstanding community service. Portia was aware of her friend's extraordinary work and once sang at a dinner for the Association's Board of Trustees.

thought the other was treating Portia badly. Portia liked to stay at Ruth Wilson's home in Moncton, New Brunswick. Wilson felt that Read kept her friend in a "permissive dictatorship." She accused the Branksome Hall principal of using Portia for free entertainment for her school functions. In some of her letters, Read complains to Wilson of "Portia's ignorance" and "Dr. Vinci's lack of cooperation." Vinci sometimes writes that he thought Portia wasn't working hard or being responsible enough.

If Portia had any idea of these private letters, it would have been very confusing to know who was her friend. It must have been difficult for her not to feel the stress of being a star. All these things happened as the war ended, the world was different and people's musical tastes shifted. Classical music was becoming less popular. Portia knew it was time for a change.

Portia the Music Teacher

GINA CIGNA

Genevieve "Gina" Cigna was born in Paris in 1900. Her career as a soprano began in 1927 and took her to Italy and around the world, playing over fifty roles. Sometimes her performances were quite dramatic. Once, when she was singing an opera in Buenos Aires, she threw herself from the top of the "Castel Saint Angelo", but found that there was no mat to land on! She finished the performance with a bleeding head. Cigna's stage career ended after a car accident in 1947. She was, however, able to teach and did so in several different countries, including Canada. Cigna lived to be more than one hundred years old, and died in 2001. She is remembered by opera fans everywhere.

With no new tours in sight, Portia decided to leave the stage for a while and approach singing from another angle—as a teacher. In the early 1950s, Portia returned to Toronto. She continued to study music with noted teachers, sopranos Gina Cigna and Irene Jessner, at the Royal Conservatory in Toronto. She taught some classes at Branksome Hall, the school of her patron, Edith Read. Portia also set up her own studio, where she taught private lessons.

When Brooke Forbes was about twelve years old, she remembers skipping excitedly to her singing lessons at Branksome Hall. Brooke already knew her teacher, Portia. She knew her teacher was "important", but she wasn't scared of her. Portia had stayed at Brooke's grandmother's boarding house when she first moved to Toronto. Grandmother Daisy's boarding house was popular with artists and performers. Brooke remembers that the house was always full of "characters"— her father's left-wing buddies; her "grandmother's friends, little old retired ladies"; gamblers and card players. Portia could get along with anybody

Brooke Forbes as a child

because "she loved to laugh. She hung out in the kitchen as she got along well with my grandmother," Brooke recalls.

"Portia was a really, really good teacher," Brooke enthuses. She could be quite warm and smiled with her student over little jokes. When they were working, Portia placed emphasis on "stance," the way I held myself," she explains. Brooke admits that she had bad posture, which used to drive her teacher "crazy." Portia had "fantastic posture." Like everyone who met Portia, Brooke notes her poise and presence.

Portia taught her young pupil without pressuring her. "She helped me get the maximum out of what I had," Brooke asserts. Although Brooke was a folk singer for a while, music was not to be her main career path, and she became a producer with the Canadian Broadcasting Corporation, CBC Radio. Brooke Forbes has happy memories of being a little girl with pigtails skipping off to music lessons. Portia was able to make her love of music grow.

On to Greater Glory

The move to Toronto in 1952 brought Portia closer to some members of her family. She was happy to have her brother, Jack, pop into her studio on his way home from work on Friday nights. She loved getting together for Christmas and seeing her nephews and nieces in Toronto or going back home whenever she could. This was important to her, as she was getting sicker and sicker.

Her younger sister, Yvonne, is sure that Portia left the concert stage because of poor health. "She was ill, but she didn't want to tell people," Yvonne affirms. One day in 1955, Yvonne herself was in the hospital in Nova Scotia. Her mother came and told her, "Vonnie, I'm going to have to leave you in the hands of the Lord. Portia needs me." Izie went to Toronto to be with Portia, who had a very serious cancer operation. Portia's health never fully returned, but she bravely continued to teach and do some singing.

There was still one of the most famous moments in her career left to play. On October 6, 1964, Portia gave a command performance before Queen Elizabeth and Prince Philip in Charlottetown, Prince Edward Island. There were only a few more concerts

Izie White, Portia's mother

Portia taking a bow at one of her last concerts

after that. The last one was in Ottawa for the Baptist Federation of Churches, in July 1967. Portia's stage career ended when she took her last bow in front of Baptist churchgoers, the same sort of audience who had first heard her sing.

Portia's battle with cancer grew worse. On February 13, 1968, her life ended with song. Her mother and those members of her family who could be there gathered around. They softly sang "I don't care what you used to be, I know what you are today," from one of her favourite songs. She would not have wanted it any other way.

Portia's Legacy

PORTIA WHITE PRIZE AWARD WINNERS

This award is given to vocalists with exceptional potential.

2002 Allison Bent
2001 Stacey Fraser
2000 Allison Bent
1999 Jennifer Farrell
1998 Heather MacKay
1993 Kathleen Flynn
1988 Pamela MacDonald
1986 Janice Jackson
1985 Carole Anne Latimer

If you look at the stars who have brightened the sky of Canadian entertainment, you will see how Portia has made some of their lights shine more strongly. She was the teacher of well-known performers Lorne Greene, Dinah Christie, Don Francks, Judy Lander and Anne Marie Moss. Portia had proven to this generation of entertainers that they didn't need to study in Europe to be successful.

Many honours have been given this woman. Canada Post has issued a Portia White stamp. The Nova Scotia Talent Trust has a scholarship called the Portia White Award for a person showing "exceptional potential as a vocalist." Nova Scotia also has an important award, created in 1995, called the Portia White Prize. In 1997, the Historic Sites and Monuments Board unveiled a plaque in Truro, the town of Portia's birth, which declared Portia White to be a person of historic significance. She is the first Canadian woman of African descent to receive this designation. Although Portia never put out a recording during her life, her brother Bill and his wife Vivian made a record of some live concert tapes after her death. The money from the sales of the record went to buy books for the Halifax Public Library. Recently, for the joy of listeners everywhere, there is a CD made by

Portia in profile in Panama City during her South American tour in 1946

her family. All of these things pay tribute to a girl who was determined to sing and the people who wanted to help her make that dream come true.

"First you dream and then you lace up your boots," Portia believed. She had many obstacles to overcome, but Portia was determined to have her dream.

She proved to the world that Canadians of every different background have talent to share. Indeed, the future changed for the better the day Portia White decided to make singing her career.

This memorial tree sculpture of Portia White by artist Bruce Wood is in Truro, Nova Scotia, at the Zion Baptist Church.

Portia White's Life and Times

1911   Portia May White is born, June 24, in Truro, Nova Scotia.

1917   She sings solos in church at age six.

1919   Her father, Reverend White, returns from World War I. The family moves to Halifax. Nova Scotia.

1929   After graduating from high school and briefly attending Dalhousie University, Portia becomes a teacher. She is eighteen.

1935, 1937, 1938
          Portia wins the Helen Campbell Kennedy silver cup.
She sings wherever and whenever she can in Halifax.

1939-1945 Canada participates in World War II.

1939   The Halifax Ladies Musical Club awards Portia a scholarship.
She begins studies with Dr. Ernesto Vinci.

1941   Portia gives her first concert in Toronto with the help of Edith Read and the Branksome Hall Alumnae. Portia signs an artist's contract and resigns as a school teacher.

1942-1944 She tours to different cities across Canada.

1944   Portia has a successful concert at Town Hall in New York city in March. She receives financial help from the Portia White Fund in May.

1946   She tours the West Indies, Latin and South America

1952   After leaving the full-time concert stage, Portia teaches voice in Toronto.

1955   Portia has an operation for cancer.

1964   Portia sings before Queen Elizabeth and Prince Philip.

1968   On February 13, Portia dies at age fifty-seven.

About the Author

lian goodall has had an interest in sharing stories since she first made up poems for her little sisters. She has a degree in history from the University of Guelph, in Ontario, where part of her studies focused on racism in Victorian children's literature. It is little surprise that she chose a related theme for her third biography for young people. lian writes Canadian children's book reviews which can be viewed at her website at www.liangoodall.com. She currently lives in Ottawa, Ontario.

Photo by Jared Will

Selected Resources Consulted by the author:

Nova Scotia Archives
Black Cultural Centre for Nova Scotia
Branksome Hall Archives
York University Archives
Ontario Black Historical Association

Honour Before Glory ©2001 a film by Anthony Sherwood Productions
Think on Me ©2000, a film by Sylvia Hamilton
www.ac.wwu.ed/~jay/pages/pwhite.html
www.sen.parl.gc.ca/doliver//Speeches/E960430.asp

Interviews and/or correspondence between lian goodall and the following: Brooke Forbes, Nancy Oliver Mackenzie, Walter Scott, Chris White, George White, Jay White, Lorne White, Vivian White, Yvonne White.

Portia White gave a number of interviews during her life for newspapers, magazines, radio and television. She also wrote letters, which remain as a record of her thoughts. Quotes are taken from these sources.

ACKNOWLEDGEMENTS

From the author:
With deep thanks to: Helen Arenburg, Nova Scotia Fruit Growers' Association; Henry Bishop, Black Cultural Centre of Nova Scotia; Brainerd Blyden-Taylor, Markus Brueggergosman and Measha Brueggergosman; Neil Carter; Ontario Ministry of Agriculture and Food; Jane Chartley, Atlantic Blue Cross Care; Derek Cooke for research help and the idea; Lynn Duquette, Nova Scotia Department of Education; Jean Edwards; Jordan Elsey; Brooke Forbes; Helen Goodall; Peter Guildford, Nova Scotia Talent Trust; Philip Hartling and Garry Shutlak, Nova Scotia Archives and Records Management; Sandra Hurlburt; Beverly Nightingale, Dalhousie University; Karen Reed; Walter Scott; Cindy Snell and Penny Elliott, Branksome Hall Archives; Elenor Peterson and Sally Houston, Ontario Black History Association Archives; Dr. Jay White; members of the White family—George Elliot Clarke, Nancy Oliver MacKenzie Oliver, Senator Don Oliver; Anthony Sherwood, Chris White, George White, Lorne White, Vivian White, Yvonne White. A very special thanks to the editors at Napoleon Publishing, who have believed in this project and graciously fostered it for some time.

From the editors:
The editors wish to thank lian goodall and Andrea Knight for their extensive work on the photo research and permissions for this book.

Photo and Art Credits